God's Plan for Me

by
Judy Hull Moore

Edited by Delores Shimmin

Library of Congress Cataloging in Publication Data

Moore, Judy Hull.
  God's plan for me.

    SUMMARY: Eyes, nose, tongue, ears, hands, hair—all are gifts of God which I must use well and take good care of.
    1. Children—Religious life. 2. Responsibility—Juvenile literature. [1. Senses and sensation]   I. Shimmin, Delores.   II. Title.
QV4571.2.M63   248.8 '2   80-17328
ISBN 0-8024-3064-3

MOODY PRESS●CHICAGO

©1976, by
A Beka Book Publications

Moody Press Edition, 1980

All rights reserved

God made me.

When I was a baby, I did not
    know much about God's world.
Now I am bigger.
God plans for me to learn more
    about His world.

> *I will praise Thee for I am*
> *fearfully and wonderfully made.*
> —Psalm 139:14

God gave me my eyes.

I can see many
   things.
I use my eyes
   to read, to work,
and to play.

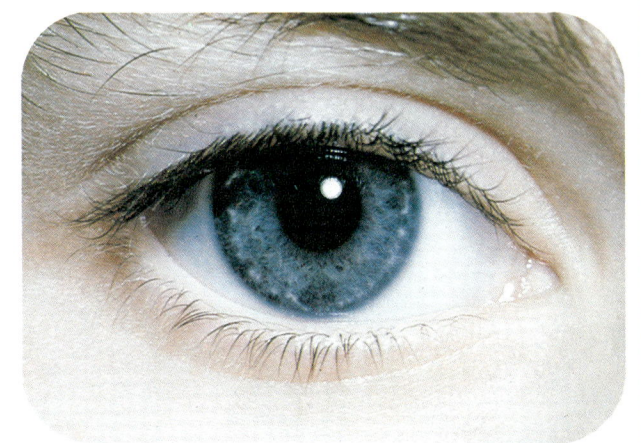

Courtesy Carolina Biological Supply Company

Color me.

O LORD, how great are Thy works! Psalm 92:5

God gave me my nose.

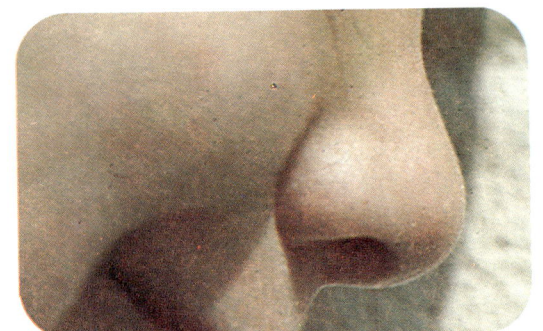

I can smell ...
    ... flowers.
    ... food.
    ... skunks.
    ... smoke.

I use my nose
    to keep me safe.

Color me.

God gave me my tongue.

I can taste something…
> …bitter.
> …sour.
> …salty.
> …sweet.

My tongue helps me to speak.
It is very little, but what it says can make others sad or happy.

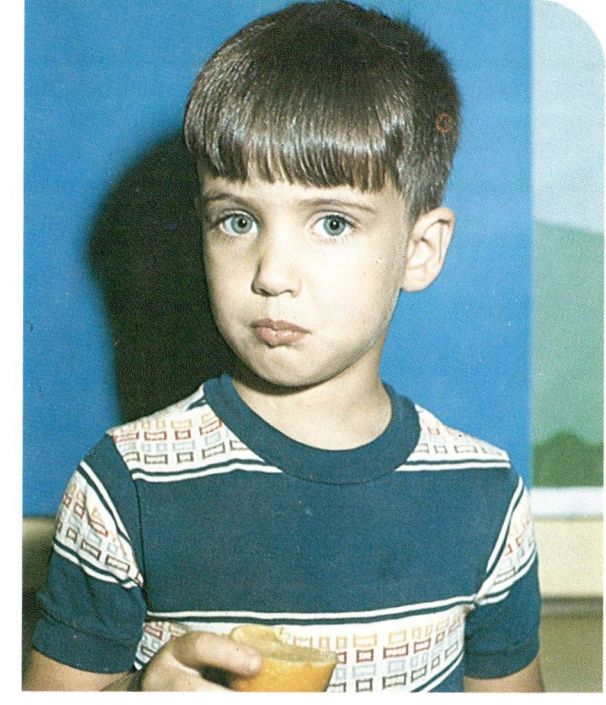

God gave me my ears.

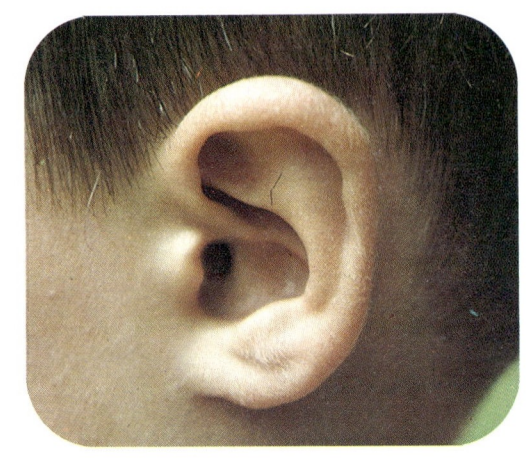

I can hear…
…my alarm clock.
…a horn honk.
…my mother call good-bye.
…my teacher at school.

Color me.

God gave me my hands.

I can hold things.
I can write.
I can get dressed.
I can help Mommy.

God gave me my hair.

Some hair is straight.
Some hair is fine.
Some hair is thick.
Some hair is curly.

Color my hair brown.

God wants me to keep clean.

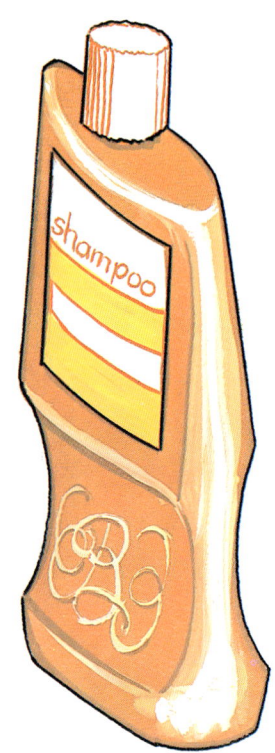

I need to…

…take a bath.   …brush my teeth.

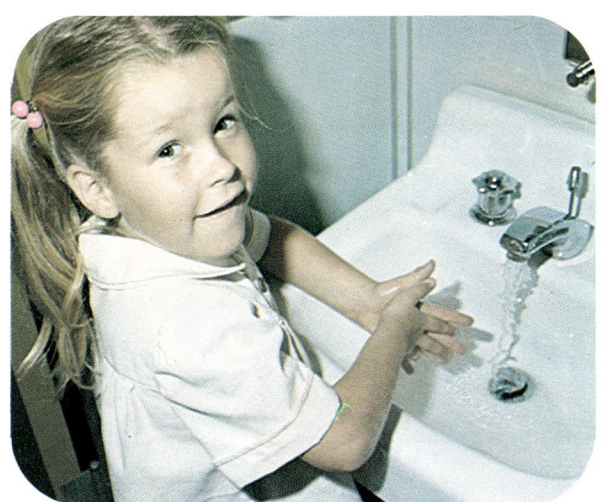
…wash my hands.

…wash my hair.

…change my clothes.

…comb my hair.

God wants me to grow.

I can grow if I ...
   ...get a good night's sleep.
   ...eat good meals.
   ...exercise.
   ...get fresh air and sunshine.

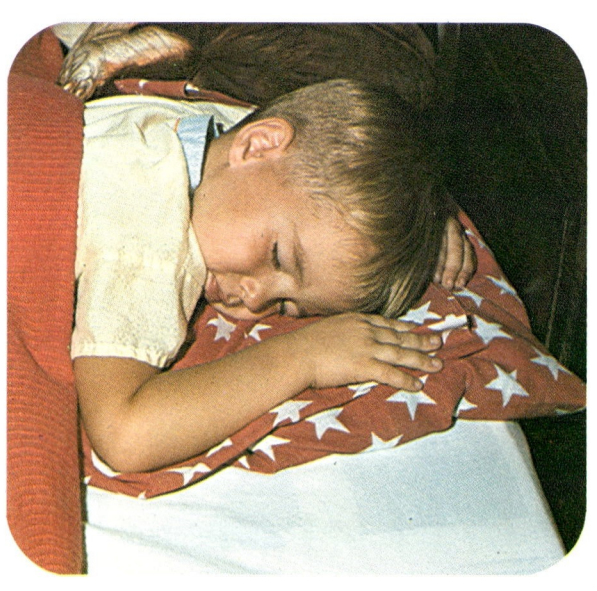

I Can Be Anyone

I can
    Jump as a robin
I can
    Hum as a bee
I can
    Hop on a twig
As a chick-a-dee-dee!

I can
    Run as a red fox
I can
    Buzz as a fly—
I can be Anyone!
But no one
    Can Be I!

—Adele H. Seronde—

Thank you, God, for making me.